Smart Alec's

KNOCK KNOCK

KNOCK!
= KNOCK!

= WHO'S THERE?

= SMART ALEC!

= PUSH OFF!

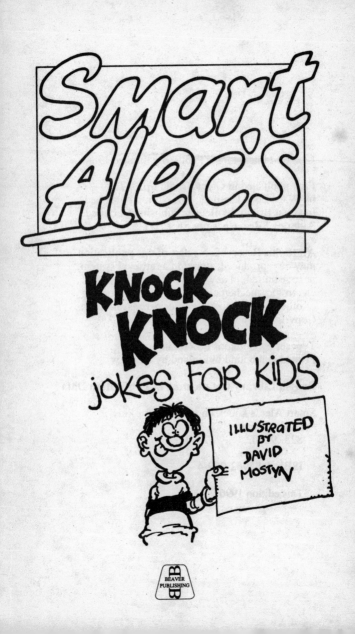

Smart Alec's

KNOCK KNOCK

jokes FOR KIDS

ILLUSTRATED BY DAVID MOSTYN

BEAVER PUBLISHING

© World International Publishing Limited 1988

First published in Great Britain in 1987
by Ward Lock Limited. This edition published
in Great Britain by Beaver Publishing Limited,
Alderley Edge, Cheshire SK9 7DT

Typeset by Columns of Reading
Printed and bound in Finland by UPC Oy

British Library Cataloguing in Publication Data

Smart Alec´s knock knock jokes for kids.
  I. Alec, *Smart*
  828´.91402   PZ8.7

  ISBN 1-85962-009-4

  This edition 1996

Knock, knock.
Who's there?
Nan.
Nan who?
Nan so deaf as those who don't want to hear.

Knock, knock.
Who's there?
Peg.
Peg who?
Peg your pardon, I've forgotten.

Knock, knock.
Who's there?
Prue.
Prue who?
Proof of the pudding is in the eating.

Knock, knock.
Who's there?
Ray.
Ray who?
Rain in Spain stays mainly on the plain.

Knock, knock.
Who's there?
Sal.
Sal who?
'S alarming, that's what it is.

Knock, knock.
Who's there?
Tim.
Tim who?
Timpossible to tell you.

Knock, knock.
Who's there?
Duke.
Duke who?
Duke come here often?

Knock, knock.
Who's there?
Tom.
Tom who?
Tom A Tosoup.

COR—A NEW PLANET!

Knock, knock.
Who's there?
Una.
Una who?
You nursing a bad tooth?

Knock, knock.
Who's there?
Val.
Val who?
Val, you ought to know by now.

Knock, knock.
Who's there?
Zoe.
Zoe who?
So 'e looks like Bowie.

Knock, knock.
Who's there?
Sue.
Sue who?
Sooner or later, I'll tell you.

START THE FLIP AT THE BACK!

THAT'S ALL FOR NOW FANS!

Knock, knock.
Who's there?
Sid.
Sid who?
'S idiotic, that's who it is.

Knock, knock.
Who's there?
Roy.
Roy who?
Roistering, rollicking me.

Knock, knock.
Who's there?
Mary.
Mary who?
Mary Christmas to all our readers.

Knock, knock.
Who's there?
Lionel.
Lionel who?
Lie an' I'll give you a tanning.

Knock, knock.
Who's there?
Winston.
Winston who?
Win some, lose some.

Knock, knock.
Who's there?
Selina.
Selina who?
So leaner meat is better for you.

Knock, knock.
Who's there?
Ian.
Ian who?
'E an awkward customer?

Knock, knock.
Who's there?
Jan.
Jan who?
January, February, June and July.

Knock, knock.
Who's there?
Jim.
Jim who?
J'imagine I'm going to tell you?

Knock, knock.
Who's there?
Joe.
Joe who?
Joking apart, I've forgotten.

Knock, knock.
Who's there?
Joy.
Joy who?
J'oil your bike regularly?

BOY - IT MUST BE A PLANET FULL OF JOKES

Knock, knock.
Who's there?
Kay.
Kay who?
Cavewoman like caveman.

Knock, knock.
Who's there?
Ken.
Ken who?
Ken't you guess?

Knock, knock.
Who's there?
Kim.
Kim who?
Kim up and see me some time.

Knock, knock.
Who's there?
Kit.
Kit who?
Kit out of it!

THAT'S ALL FOR NOW FANS!

Knock, knock.
Who's there?
Len.
Len who?
Lend me a fiver?

Knock, knock.
Who's there?
Melinda.
Melinda who?
Me lend a fiver? Not likely.

Knock, knock.
Who's there?
Liz.
Liz who?
Liz is just ridiculous.

Knock, knock.
Who's there?
Lyn.
Lyn who?
Linger a little longer.

COME ON DOWN LADS—IT'S ALL JOKES AND THINGS

Knock, knock.
Who's there?
Max.
Max who?
Max very little difference who it is.

Knock, knock.
Who's there?
Maxie.
Maxie who?
Maximum with maxidad.

Knock, knock.
Who's there?
May.
May who?
Made your mistake in asking.

Knock, knock.
Who's there?
Meg.
Meg who?
Meg an omelette without eggs.

Knock, knock.
Who's there?
Guy.
Guy who?
Guy do you ask?

TWANG!

Knock, knock.
Who's there?
Patrick.
Patrick who?
Patrically an idiot.

Knock, knock.
Who's there?
Olive.
Olive who?
A living doll.

Knock, knock.
Who's there?
Martha.
Martha who?
Ma thirsts for a Coca Cola.

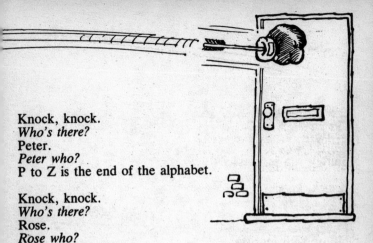

Knock, knock.
Who's there?
Peter.
Peter who?
P to Z is the end of the alphabet.

Knock, knock.
Who's there?
Rose.
Rose who?
Roes on toast for two.

Knock, knock.
Who's there?
Celia.
Celia who?
Seal yer envelopes with sticky tape.

Knock, knock.
Who's there?
Shirley.
Shirley who?
Shirley you've guessed?

Knock, knock.
Who's there?
Philip.
Philip who?
Fill up with four-star.

Knock, knock.
Who's there?
Juno.
Juno who?
Juno what I know?

Knock, knock.
Who's there?
Michael.
Michael who?
My collection's better than yours.

Knock, knock.
Who's there?
Mona.
Mona who?
Mown a lawn for fifty pence?

Knock, knock.
Who's there?
Thora.
Thora who?
Thaw a cube of ice with hot water.

Knock, knock.
Who's there?
Margie.
Margie who?
Margie—rine or butter?

Knock, knock.
Who's there?
Douglas.
Douglas who?
Dug lashings of spuds up.

Knock, knock.
Who's there?
Leopold.
Leopold who?
Leo poled his punt up river.

Knock, knock.
Who's there?
Amy.
Amy who?
Eh? Me and several others.

Knock, knock.
Who's there?
Annie.
Annie who?
Annie body here seen Kelly?

Knock, knock.
Who's there?
Ben.
Ben who?
Ben to the cinema lately?

Knock, knock.
Who's there?
Alf.
Alf who?
All fares, please.

Knock, knock.
Who's there?
Earl.
Earl who?
Early enough for you?

Knock, knock.
Who's there?
Ella.
Ella who?
'Ell of a row going on.

Knock, knock.
Who's there?
Dora.
Dora who?
Dora funny face on the blackboard.

MR. MACBRAGGLE

Knock, knock.
Who's there?
Dick.
Dick who?
Dictate your name more slowly.

Knock, knock.
Who's there?
Dawn.
Dawn who?
Door not quite shut is ajar.

Knock, knock.
Who's there?
Davie.
Davie who?
Day ve met the rabbi.

Knock, knock.
Who's there?
Clem.
Clem who?
Clem up and say nothing.

Knock, knock.
Who's there?
Bill.
Bill who?
Belonging to next door?

Knock, knock.
Who's there?
Beth.
Beth who?
Bether late than never.

Knock, knock.
Who's there?
Bart.
Bart who?
Bartender or beer-drinker?

Knock, knock.
Who's there?
Amos.
Amos who?
A most respected person.

Knock, knock.
Who's there?
Adam.
Adam who?
A damp squib on November 5th.

Knock, knock.
Who's there?
Emile.
Emile who?
A military escort.

Knock, knock.
Who's there?
Eric.
Eric who?
A rickshaw driver.

Knock, knock.
Who's there?
Marion.
Marion who?
Marry an idiot and repent at leisure.

Knock, knock.
Who's there?
Gordon.
Gordon who?
Gordon Bleu cookery expert.

Knock, knock.
Who's there?
Tessa.
Tessa who?
Tess a coin to decide it.

Knock, knock.
Who's there?
Erica.
Erica who?
A ricochet off the wall.

Knock, knock.
Who's there?
Anita.
Anita who?
A neater way of putting it.

Knock, knock.
Who's there?
Harry.
Harry who?
Harry on down to my house.

Knock, knock.
Who's there?
Nat.
Nat who?
Nat going to tell you!

GOSH CHAPS—HE MUST BE THE JOKE WRITER—LOOK, HE'S THINKING OF A JOKE!

I DON'T UNDERSTAND THESE JOKES!

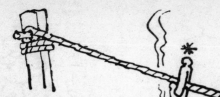

Knock, knock.
Who's there?
Ned.
Ned who?
Ned-you-can-ezzer.

Knock, knock.
Who's there?
Pam.
Pam who?
Pamission granted.

Knock, knock.
Who's there?
Sam.
Sam who?
'S amazing, that's who it is.

Knock, knock.
Who's there?
Isabel.
Isabel who?
Is a belfry a batty place?

A REFERENCE TO ME AGAIN - FOLKS

*** READERS PLEASE NOTE:
THE REEKING SOCK IN
"SMART ALEC'S BEASTLY
JOKES FOR KIDS" - HAS
NOW BEEN WASHED!**

Knock, knock.
Who's there?
Eileen.
Eileen who?
I leaned over and fell.

NO, SHE DIDN'T — I PUSHED HER

Knock, knock.
Who's there?
Ida.
Ida who?
I'd a hoe but lost it in the garden.

Knock, knock.
Who's there?
Ivor.
Ivor who?
I've 'eard you're no friend of mine.

Knock, knock.
Who's there?
Francis.
Francis who?
France is the other side of the Channel.

Knock, knock.
Who's there?
Nora.
Nora who?
Gnaw a bone if you have any teeth.

Knock, knock.
Who's there?
Flora.
Flora who?
Floor a smart-alec with this question.

Knock, knock.
Who's there?
Phyllis.
Phyllis who?
Philistine.

Knock, knock.
Who's there?
Walter.
Walter who?
Wall to wall carpet.

Knock, knock.
Who's there?
Robin.
Robin who?
Robin the rich to give to the poor.

LOOK LADS —
AN INVISIBLE MAN
IN A SOCK

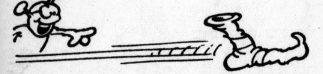

Knock, knock.
Who's there?
Rosa.
Rosa who?
Rows a boat around the harbour.

Knock, knock.
Who's there?
Abel.
Abel who?
A bull and a cow had a row.

Knock, knock.
Who's there?
Abie.
Abie who?
Eh, be more gentle!

Knock, knock.
Who's there?
Adam.
Adam who?
Add 'em or subtract 'em?

Knock, knock.
Who's there?
Aldo.
Aldo who?
All donations welcome.

I JUST DON'T UNDERSTAND ANYTHING

WEEP
HOWL
SOB.

Knock, knock.
Who's there?
Alma.
Alma who?
'Ell, Ma, this is uneatable.

Knock, knock.
Who's there?
Amos.
Amos who?
A mosquito is the same as a gnat.

Knock, knock.
Who's there?
Andy.
Andy who?
And 'e never said thank you.

Knock, knock.
Who's there?
Alan.
Alan who?
A lantern burning for my wandering boy.

Knock, knock.
Who's there?
Violet.
Violet who?
Vile it may be, if it's strong medicine.

Knock, knock.
Who's there?
Harry.
Harry who?
Haricot beans or runners for you?

Knock, knock.
Who's there?
Wilbur.
Wilbur who?
We'll burn all the guys on November 5th.

Knock, knock.
Who's there?
Yvonne.
Yvonne who?
'Eave on that rope, lads.

Knock, knock.
Who's there?
Abigail.
Abigail who?
A big gale or a storm in a teacup?

Knock, knock.
Who's there?
Barbara.
Barbara who?
Baa-baa a sheepish sound.

Knock, knock.
Who's there?
Bernard.
Bernard who?
Burn 'ardly anything and keep fuel bills down.

Knock, knock.
Who's there?
Bridget.
Bridget who?
Bridge? It's got nothing on poker!

Knock, knock.
Who's there?
Elinor.
Elinor who?
A linoleum salesman sold me this flooring.

Knock, knock.
Who's there?
Jessica.
Jessica who?
Je-seek a new boyfriend?

Knock, knock.
Who's there?
Gill.
Gill who?
Jilted lover seeks revenge.

Knock, knock.
Who's there?
Milly.
Milly who?
Milliners may be mad as hatters.

Knock, knock.
Who's there?
Maxwell.
Maxwell who?
Mac's well but Annie's poorly.

Knock, knock.
Who's there?
Matilda.
Matilda who?
Met 'ilda after dark in the park.

Knock, knock.
Who's there?
Deirdre.
Deirdre who?
Dear dreams or sweet dreams.

Knock, knock.
Who's there?
Chris.
Chris who?
Christmas comes but once a year.

Knock, knock.
Who's there?
Lucille.
Lucille who?
Loose 'eel and a worn-out sole.

Knock, knock.
Who's there?
Lucinda.
Lucinda who?
Lou's in dirty surroundings.

Knock, knock.
Who's there?
Margaret.
Margaret who?
My regret for my mistake.

Knock, knock.
Who's there?
Vanessa.
Vanessa who?
Van essential for local deliveries.

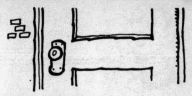

Knock, knock.
Who's there?
Giselle.
Giselle who?
She's elegant and well-groomed.

Knock, knock.
Who's there?
Heather.
Heather who?
Heather another one on me.

Knock, knock.
Who's there?
Nicholas.
Nicholas who?
Nick a lass and pinch a boy.

Knock, knock.
Who's there?
Solomon.
Solomon who?
Solemn on this serious occasion.

Knock, knock.
Who's there?
Harriet.
Harriet who?
Hurry it along there.

Knock, knock.
Who's there?
Trudy.
Trudy who?
True delight from Turkey.

Knock, knock.
Who's there?
Heidi.
Heidi who?
High dinner or high tea?

Knock, knock.
Who's there?
Sarah.
Sarah who?
Sarah way out of this maze?

Knock, knock.
Who's there?
Christy.
Christy who?
Chris, tea or coffee?

Knock, knock.
Who's there?
Amanda.
Amanda who?
A man demanded to see her.

Knock, knock.
Who's there?
Felicity.
Felicity who?
Fill a city with skyscrapers.

Knock, knock.
Who's there?
Benjamin.
Benjamin who?
Been jammin' the blues?

Knock, knock.
Who's there?
Leon.
Leon who?
Leigh-on-Sea is near Southend.

Knock, knock.
Who's there?
Julie.
Julie who?
Ju-leak official secrets?

Knock, knock.
Who's there?
Marigold.
Marigold who?
Marry Goldfinger, Mrs Midas?

Knock, knock.
Who's there?
Beatrice.
Beatrice who?
Be a Tricity saleswoman.

Knock, knock.
Who's there?
Ariadne.
Ariadne who?
'Arry 'ad next to nothing on.

Knock, knock.
Who's there?
Adeline.
Adeline who?
'Ad a line of washing out in the rain.

Knock, knock.
Who's there?
Benedict.
Benedict who?
Benny dictated all his letters.

Knock, knock.
Who's there?
Milly.
Milly who?
Millions of men can't be wrong.

Knock, knock.
Who's there?
Wyndham.
Wyndham who?
Wind 'im with a low blow.

Knock, knock.
Who's there?
Fenella.
Fenella who?
Fun a lad has with her!

Knock, knock.
Who's there?
Wallis.
Wallis who?
Well as can be expected.

Knock, knock.
Who's there?
Jeff.
Jeff who?
J-effer see such a sight?

Knock, knock.
Who's there?
Humphrey.
Humphrey who?
Hum free but there's a charge for singing.

Knock, knock.
Who's there?
Terence.
Terence who?
Terence of rain caused the flooding.

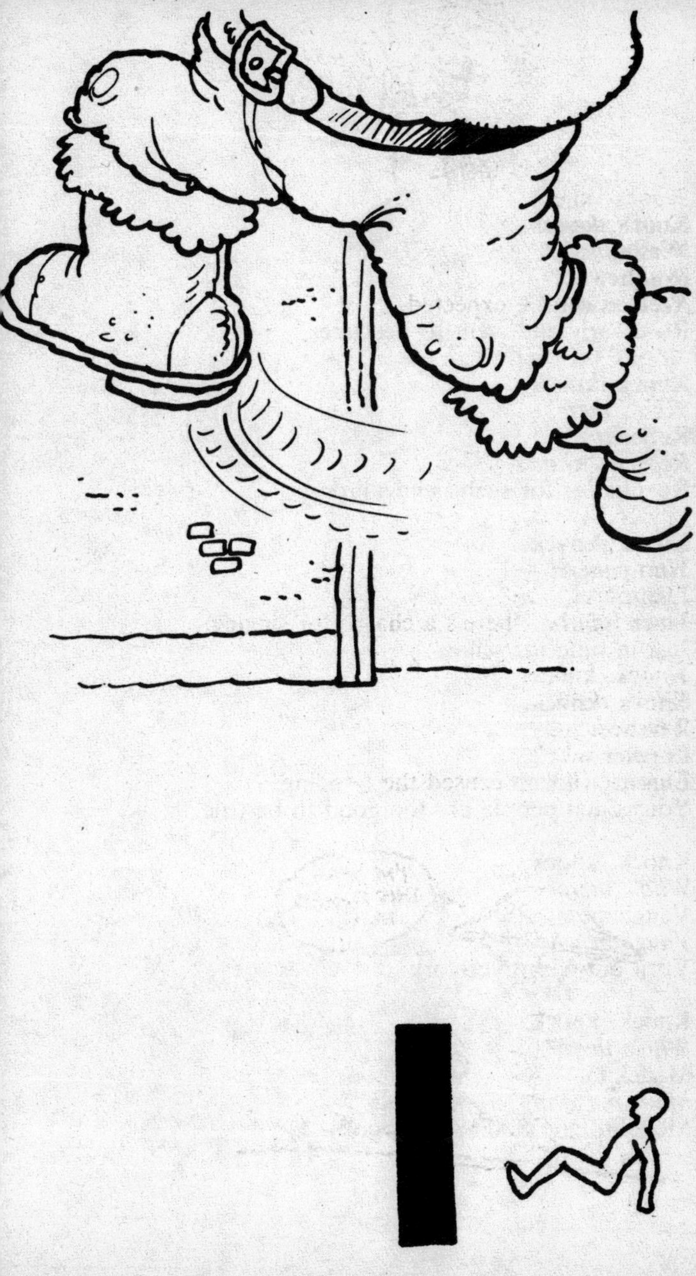

Knock, knock.
Who's there?
Rosalie.
Rosalie who?
Rose early and went to bed late.

Knock, knock.
Who's there?
Rebecca.
Rebecca who?
Rebuke 'er for such behaviour.

Knock, knock.
Who's there?
Justin.
Justin who?
Just in time for school.

Knock, knock.
Who's there?
Eugene.
Eugene who?
You genial people are too good to be true.

Knock, knock.
Who's there?
Vaughan.
Vaughan who?
Vorn out with over-vork.

Knock, knock.
Who's there?
Madeline.
Madeline who?
Meddlin' and fiddlin' the books.

Knock, knock.
Who's there?
Matt.
Matt who?
Matinee idol the ladies love.

Knock, knock.
Who's there?
Julian.
Julian who?
Jew lie on a mattress?

Knock, knock.
Who's there?
Florrie.
Florrie who?
Florida is the place for sunbathing.

Knock, knock.
Who's there?
Yolande.
Yolande who?
Yo land at Gatwick from Spain?

Knock, knock.
Who's there?
Ottilie.
Ottilie who?
Ottilie enchanting, you are.

Knock, knock.
Who's there?
William.
William who?
Will yam cook up as a vegetable?

Knock, knock.
Who's there?
Noah.
Noah who?
Know a better way of doing it?

Knock, knock.
Who's there?
Geoffrey.
Geoffrey who?
J-free that prisoner who was innocent?

Knock, knock.
Who's there?
Natalie.
Natalie who?
Naturlie, we're delighted to see you.

Knock, knock.
Who's there?
Stan.
Stan who?
'S-tan I got in Malta.

Knock, knock.
Who's there?
Lorraine.
Lorraine who?
Low rainfall in East Anglia.

Knock, knock.
Who's there?
Priscilla.
Priscilla who?
Precisely my own feelings.

Knock, knock.
Who's there?
Jock.
Jock who?
J-occupy all this house?

Knock, knock.
Who's there?
Jules.
Jules who?
Jewels and gems and semi-precious stones.

Knock, knock.
Who's there?
Maximilian.
Maximilian who?
Makes a millionaire look poor!

Knock, knock.
Who's there?
Esme.
Esme who?
Es many as possible.

Knock, knock.
Who's there?
Gwendolyn.
Gwendolyn who?
Gwen dolin' out the food is so slow.

Knock, knock.
Who's there?
Wilhelmina.
Wilhelmina who?
Will Hell mean a fire in every room?

Knock, knock.
Who's there?
Stephanie.
Stephanie who?
Steph on it and we may get there in time.

Knock, knock.
Who's there?
Nicolette.
Nicolette who?
Nick a letter and steam it open.

Knock, knock.
Who's there?
Jacquetta.
Jacquetta who?
Jack ate a sour apple and had tummy-ache.

Knock, knock.
Who's there?
Millicent.
Millicent who?
Mill 'e sent was full of pepper.

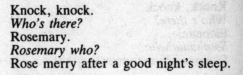

Knock, knock.
Who's there?
Rosemary.
Rosemary who?
Rose merry after a good night's sleep.

Knock, knock.
Who's there?
Rosie.
Rosie who?
Row secretly out of port.

Knock, knock.
Who's there?
Marmaduke.
Marmaduke who?
Mama, do cut the cake now.

Knock, knock.
Who's there?
Theodore.
Theodore who?
The odour is horrible.

Knock, knock.
Who's there?
Elspeth.
Elspeth who?
I'll specially mention you.

Knock, knock.
Who's there?
Claudia.
Claudia who?
Clawed Ian like a cat.

Knock, knock.
Who's there?
Gregory.
Gregory who?
Grog or real ale?

Knock, knock.
Who's there?
Sybil.
Sybil who?
So billions of pounds are spent.

Knock, knock.
Who's there?
Viola.
Viola who?
Vee 'ole a putt from twenty yards, my boy.

I DRIVE PEOPLE MAD 'CAUSE I'M SO CLEVER!

Knock, knock.
Who's there?
Wanda.
Wanda who?
Wanda new friend?

Knock, knock.
Who's there?
Susie.
Susie who?
Sues easily when wronged.

Knock, knock.
Who's there?
Sonia.
Sonia who?
S' on yer own head, be it!

Knock, knock.
Who's there?
Simon.
Simon who?
So I'm on night-duty again.

Knock, knock.
Who's there?
Sandy.
Sandy who?
Sandy afternoon on the beach.

Knock, knock.
Who's there?
Sally.
Sally who?
'S-alligators I'm scared of.

Knock, knock.
Who's there?
Sadie.
Sadie who?
Say, dear, if you've had enough.

Knock, knock.
Who's there?
Rufus.
Rufus who?
Roof us over – we're getting soaked.

Knock, knock.
Who's there?
Rhoda.
Rhoda who?
Rode 'er 'orse all round 'yde Park.

Knock, knock.
Who's there?
Ralph.
Ralph who?
Ralphabetically, he's well down the list.

Knock, knock.
Who's there?
Polly.
Polly who?
Politically, just a parrot.

Knock, knock.
Who's there?
Percy.
Percy who?
Persecuted for very little reason.

Knock, knock.
Who's there?
Oona.
Oona who?
'o nursed the baby?

Knock, knock.
Who's there?
Pearl.
Pearl who?
Purr like a fat cat.

Knock, knock.
Who's there?
Paula.
Paula who?
Poor learn fast how to steal.

AUNTIE FLORA

Knock, knock.
Who's there?
Oscar.
Oscar who?
Oscar policeman.

Knock, knock.
Who's there?
Norma.
Norma who?
Nor Ma nor Pa nor Uncle Bill.

Knock, knock.
Who's there?
Norman.
Norman who?
Norman service will be resumed shortly.

Knock, knock.
Who's there?
Nicky.
Nicky who?
Knee key for those with locked leg?

NOTE FROM STARVING ARTIST. SEND ME £350. I WILL DRAW AN ACCURATE PORTRAIT OF YOUR BONCE ON ONE OF THESE PAGES.

Knock, knock.
Who's there?
Nelly.
Nelly who?
Nelly midnight, Cinderella.

Knock, knock.
Who's there?
Naomi.
Naomi who?
Neigh ominously if your horse is lame.

Knock, knock.
Who's there?
Myrna.
Myrna who?
My nerves are shot to pieces.

Knock, knock.
Who's there?
Morag.
Morag who?
More aggro in Scotland.

HAMISH MACTOOTS!

Knock, knock.
Who's there?
Moira.
Moira who?
More a fool than a knave.

Knock, knock.
Who's there?
Mitzi.
Mitzi who?
Mid-sea romance and wedding.

Knock, knock.
Who's there?
Mavis.
Mavis who?
May vistas of apple-blossom.

Knock, knock.
Who's there?
Maud.
Maud who?
More drama by the garden-gate.

HAMISH MACTOOTS
SAYS: YE GET MORE
FUR YOUR SILLER *
IN THE FAINE
JOKE BOOKIE—
OCH AYE—THE
HOOTS—THE NOO!

* SILLER = MONEY

Knock, knock.
Who's there?
Marie.
Marie who?
M' reasons are well-known.

Knock, knock.
Who's there?
Maria.
Maria who?
M'rear window is misted up.

Knock, knock.
Who's there?
Margo.
Margo who?
Mar go buy some shopping.

Knock, knock.
Who's there?
Mame.
Mame who?
May meet me tonight.

Knock, knock.
Who's there?
Madge.
Madge who?
Majority in favour.

Knock, knock.
Who's there?
Mabel.
Mabel who?
May belie all the rumours.

Knock, knock.
Who's there?
Lydia.
Lydia who?
Lid o' yer teapot's cracked.

Knock, knock.
Who's there?
Lloyd.
Lloyd who?
Lloyds or the Oval, it's still cricket.

Knock, knock.
Who's there?
Kevin.
Kevin who?
Cave in under pressure.

Knock, knock.
Who's there?
Keith.
Keith who?
Key thief can unlock your door.

Knock, knock.
Who's there?
Joyce.
Joyce who?
Joyce of the orange without additives.

Knock, knock.
Who's there?
Jimmy.
Jimmy who?
J'imitate TV personalities?

Knock, knock.
Who's there?
Jerry.
Jerry who?
J'erect that extraordinary building?

Knock, knock.
Who's there?
Jason.
Jason who?
Jason backwards and forwards.

IF ANYONE UNDERSTANDS THE JOKE
SUSPENDED ABOVE, SEND £30.50 TO
SMART ALEXANDER AND YOU WILL
BE GIVEN A FULL REFUND!

Knock, knock.
Who's there?
Janet.
Janet who?
Janitors are the same as caretakers.

Knock, knock.
Who's there?
Jacqueline.
Jacqueline who?
Jekyll and Hyde.

Knock, knock.
Who's there?
Isaac.
Isaac who?
I suck my thumb when I'm bored.

Knock, knock.
Who's there?
Inigo.
Inigo who?
In egoism I excel.

Knock, knock.
Who's there?
Honor.
Honor who?
On a clear day, you can see forever.

Knock, knock.
Who's there?
Hiram.
Hiram who?
Hire 'em, fire 'em, don't pay 'em.

Knock, knock.
Who's there?
Hilda.
Hilda who?
He'll demand to know her name.

Knock, knock.
Who's there?
Helga.
Helga who?
He'll guard her with his life.

Knock, knock.
Who's there?
Helen.
Helen who?
Hell an' high water.

HE HASN'T GOT THE LIPS FOR IT

Knock, knock.
Who's there?
Hazel.
Hazel who?
Hay zealously fed to horses.

Knock, knock.
Who's there?
Greta.
Greta who?
Greet 'er with a kiss.

Knock, knock.
Who's there?
Grace.
Grace who?
Grey's the colour of warships.

Knock, knock.
Who's there?
Ginny.
Ginny who?
G'initiate her into the club?

Knock, knock.
Who's there?
Giles.
Giles who?
Child's play to get the answer.

Knock, knock.
Who's there?
Garth.
Garth who?
Garfunkel's nephew.

Knock, knock.
Who's there?
Romeo.
Romeo who?
Row me over the river.

Knock, knock.
Who's there?
Juliet.
Juliet who?
Juliet him get away with that?

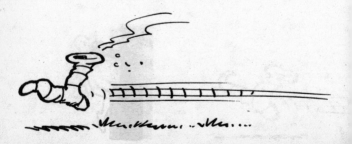

Knock, knock.
Who's there?
Portia.
Portia who?
Pour sherbet into a glass.

Knock, knock.
Who's there?
Thea.
Thea who?
The early bird catches the worm.

Knock, knock.
Who's there?
Ray.
Ray who?
Ray of sunshine.

Knock, knock.
Who's there?
Theo.
Theo who?
The Old Curiosity Shop.

Knock, knock.
Who's there?
Fred.
Fred who?
Fred this needle – I'm cross-eyed.

Knock, knock.
Who's there?
Gail.
Gail who?
Gale warning to all shipping.

Knock, knock.
Who's there?
Wendy.
Wendy who?
When d'you expect to see him?

Knock, knock.
Who's there?
Diane.
Diane who?
Dai angry when Wales lose?

Knock, knock.
Who's there?
Hugh.
Hugh who?
Huge reductions in all departments.

Knock, knock.
Who's there?
Hugo.
Hugo who?
You going away this summer?

Knock, knock.
Who's there?
Iris.
Iris who?
Irish stew and dumplings.

Knock, knock.
Who's there?
Ivan.
Ivan who?
I've angered you again.

Knock, knock.
Who's there?
Jean.
Jean who?
G an' H follow E an' F.

Knock, knock.
Who's there?
Jess.
Jess who?
Gesture of goodwill.

Knock, knock.
Who's there?
Joan.
Joan who?
Joan your own house?

Knock, knock.
Who's there?
Jess.
Jess who?
Jespect me to believe that?

Knock, knock.
Who's there?
Judy.
Judy who?
Judeliver newspapers still?

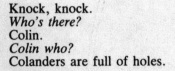

Knock, knock.
Who's there?
Colin.
Colin who?
Colanders are full of holes.

Knock, knock.
Who's there?
Kate.
Kate who?
Catering for a big party?

Knock, knock.
Who's there?
Lena.
Lena who?
Lean a bike against the wall.

Knock, knock.
Who's there?
Lisa.
Lisa who?
Lasagne for you?

Knock, knock.
Who's there?
Terry.
Terry who?
Terrible twins or tricky triplets?

Knock, knock.
Who's there?
Trixie.
Trixie who?
Tricks 'e played on 'er.

Knock, knock.
Who's there?
Charlie.
Charlie who?
Charlie that's not your boyfriend?

Knock, knock.
Who's there?
Ronnie.
Ronnie who?
Ronnie butter spreads more quickly.

Knock, knock.
Who's there?
Bob.
Bob who?
Bobbin' up and down like this.

Knock, knock.
Who's there?
Evelyn.
Evelyn who?
Evelyn all!

Knock, knock.
Who's there?
Hattie.
Hattie who?
Hattie known, he wouldn't have done it.

Knock, knock.
Who's there?
Duncan.
Duncan who?
Done Canada, now off to Japan.

Knock, knock.
Who's there?
Gideon.
Gideon who?
Giddy on the swings and roundabouts.

Knock, knock.
Who's there?
Hamish.
Hamish who?
Hey, Mishter, ish thish the way to Shishester?

Knock, knock.
Who's there?
Dwight.
Dwight who?
Dwight or wrong?

Knock, knock.
Who's there?
Dougal.
Dougal who?
Do gulls nest on icebergs?

Knock, knock.
Who's there?
Edwina.
Edwina who?
'Ad we nerve, we'd have done it.

Knock, knock.
Who's there?
Eugene.
Eugene who?
You Jean or Joyce?

Knock, knock.
Who's there?
Graham.
Graham who?
Grey hamsters or white mice?

Knock, knock.
Who's there?
Elvira.
Elvira who?
'Ell, Vera, that's not very kind.

Knock, knock.
Who's there?
Carmen.
Carmen who?
Car men don't like walking.

Knock, knock.
Who's there?
Arthur.
Arthur who?
Arthur loaf is better than none.

Knock, knock.
Who's there?
Bertha.
Bertha who?
Berth a boat in a dry dock.

Knock, knock.
Who's there?
Austin.
Austin who?
Austintatiously done.

Knock, knock.
Who's there?
Audrey.
Audrey who?
Ordering your meal now?

Knock, knock.
Who's there?
Archie.
Archie who?
Are cheeses always round?

Knock, knock.
Who's there?
Arabel.
Arabel who?
A rabble of football supporters.

Knock, knock.
Who's there?
Anthony.
Anthony who?
Anti-nuclear demo.

Knock, knock.
Who's there?
Claire.
Claire who?
Claire your throat before speaking.

Knock, knock.
Who's there?
Carrie.
Carrie who?
Carry your bags, mister?

Knock, knock.
Who's there?
Connor.
Connor who?
Connor long way past his turning.

Knock, knock.
Who's there?
Damian.
Damian who?
Day me and my mate went on holiday.

Knock, knock.
Who's there?
Denise.
Denise who?
Denise having anything to do with it.

Knock, knock.
Who's there?
Dermot.
Dermot who?
Dermatology is only skin-deep.

Knock, knock.
Who's there?
Doreen.
Doreen who?
Door Ian slammed in my face.

Knock, knock.
Who's there?
Alison.
Alison who?
Alice on a bike is quite amusing.

ALICE
PIPES

Knock, knock.
Who's there?
Amelia.
Amelia who?
A mealier-mouthed man I've never met.

Knock, knock.
Who's there?
Andrea.
Andrea who?
And rear view is of the open fields.

Knock, knock.
Who's there?
Aldous.
Aldous who?
All dust swept under the carpet.

Knock, knock.
Who's there?
Albert.
Albert who?
Alberta is in Canada.

Knock, knock.
Who's there?
Aileen.
Aileen who?
A leaning tower is in Pisa.

Knock, knock.
Who's there?
Agatha.
Agatha who?
Agatha you're not very fond of me.

Knock, knock.
Who's there?
Adrian.
Adrian who?
Atreean a bush in the front garden.

Knock, knock.
Who's there?
Oedipus.
Oedipus who?
'E dip us in the training pool?

Knock, knock.
Who's there?
Caesar.
Caesar who?
Caesar jolly good fellow.

Knock, knock.
Who's there?
Freda.
Freda who?
Freed 'er from prison.

Knock, knock.
Who's there?
Fay.
Fay who?
Faith, hope and charity.

Knock, knock.
Who's there?
Van.
Van who?
Van I vant yu, I'll call.

Knock, knock.
Who's there?
Ajax.
Ajax who?
A jack's to lift a car.

Knock, knock.
Who's there?
Dido.
Dido who?
Dai donated some blood.

Knock, knock.
Who's there?
Ava.
Ava who?
Ava good mind to leave.

Knock, knock.
Who's there?
Thor.
Thor who?
Thought I saw you in the supermarket.

ETHEL (LOVELY THING)

Knock, knock.
Who's there?
Seth.
Seth who?
'S Ethel who's my sister.

Knock, knock.
Who's there?
Cain.
Cain who?
Cain't you see through a brick wall?

Knock, knock.
Who's there?
Atlas.
Atlas who?
At Las Vegas you can gamble all night.

Knock, knock.
Who's there?
Grace.
Grace who?
Grey stones may be granite.

Knock, knock.
Who's there?
Minnie.
Minnie who?
Minestrone or mulligatawny for you?

SMART ALEXANDER'S SUPER LONG-RANGE LIPS

Knock, knock.
Who's there?
Ethelred.
Ethelred who?
Ethel reddened when kissed.

Knock, knock.
Who's there?
Moira.
Moira who?
Moiracles do happen.

Knock, knock.
Who's there?
Uriah.
Uriah who?
Uriah than I am in the ratings.

Knock, knock.
Who's there?
Apollo.
Apollo who?
A polo player.

Knock, knock.
Who's there?
Oberon
Oberon who?
Oberon the other side of the road.

Knock, knock.
Who's there?
Petula.
Petula who?
Petulaugh at all his jokes.

Knock, knock.
Who's there?
Aladdin.
Aladdin who?
A lad inspired to great deeds.

Knock, knock.
Who's there?
Jupiter.
Jupiter who?
Jupiter strong man against a weak one?

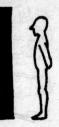

Knock, knock.
Who's there?
Titania.
Titania who?
Titter near a solemn ceremony.

Knock, knock.
Who's there?
Tristan.
Tristan who?
Tristan shout.

Knock, knock.
Who's there?
Percival.
Percival who?
Purse 'e valued very highly.

DOCTOR JIM

YOU'RE SUFFERING FROM A SURFEIT OF FRONT DOORS

Knock, knock.
Who's there?
Peter Pan.
Peter Pan who?
Pete a-panting after the marathon.

Knock, knock.
Who's there?
Alexander.
Alexander who?
Alec's under the doctor.

Knock, knock.
Who's there?
Jonah.
Jonah who?
Jonah bicycle?

Knock, knock.
Who's there?
Pandora.
Pandora who?
Pan Dora fried the fish in.

Knock, knock.
Who's there?
Aesop.
Aesop who?
Aesop to his old tricks.

Knock, knock.
Who's there?
Christopher.
Christopher who?
Chris to offer a bargain?

Knock, knock.
Who's there?
Petronella.
Petronella who?
Pet, Ron, Ella, and anyone else who's around.

Knock, knock.
Who's there?
Ham.
Ham who?
Hampstead and Highgate.

I CAN'T LET MY SOCK SEE ME LIKE THIS

Knock, knock.
Who's there?
Job.
Job who?
Joe burped after a meal.

Knock, knock.
Who's there?
Lot.
Lot who?
Lot on your plate?

Knock, knock.
Who's there?
Ahab.
Ahab who?
A habit you want to break.

Knock, knock.
Who's there?
Esau.
Esau who?
Ease or hard work?

Knock, knock.
Who's there?
Jude.
Jude who?
Jude a unseen circumstances.

Knock, knock.
Who's there?
Levi.
Levi who?
Lee vies with Lou.

Knock, knock.
Who's there?
Luke.
Luke who?
Luke both ways before crossing.

Knock, knock.
Who's there?
Mark.
Mark who?
Ma can't cook for toffee.

STICK TO BONES-MAN

Knock, knock.
Who's there?
Saul.
Saul who?
Saul over and done with.

Knock, knock.
Who's there?
Shem.
Shem who?
Shemple Shimon.

Knock, knock.
Who's there?
Aaron.
Aaron who?
'Air on chest means strength in arms.

Knock, knock.
Who's there?
Enoch.
Enoch who?
Inoculated against everything.

Knock, knock.
Who's there?
Herod.
Herod who?
Hair oddly waved.

Knock, knock.
Who's there?
Hosea.
Hosea who?
Hosea and use the watering-can there.

Knock, knock.
Who's there?
Isaac.
Isaac who?
Isaacly what I mean.

Knock, knock.
Who's there?
Judas.
Judas who?
Judash about like this all the time?

Knock, knock.
Who's there?
Micah.
Micah who?
My car goes faster than yours.

Knock, knock.
Who's there?
Moses.
Moses who?
Mows estates with a motor-mower.

Knock, knock.
Who's there?
Silas.
Silas who?
Silence is golden.

Knock, knock.
Who's there?
Titus.
Titus who?
Tight as a lord.

Knock, knock.
Who's there?
Uriel.
Uriel who?
You real or unreal?

Knock, knock.
Who's there?
Isaiah.
Isaiah who?
Eyes 'igher with high-brows.

Knock, knock.
Who's there?
Judith.
Judith who?
Judither about like this all the time?

Knock, knock.
Who's there?
Nathan.
Nathan who?
Nay, Thanet is not in Surrey.

Knock, knock.
Who's there?
Samuel.
Samuel who?
Samuel keep, some you'll chuck out.

Knock, knock.
Who's there?
Absalom.
Absalom who?
Absalomutely the right thing to do.

Knock, knock.
Who's there?
Ephraim.
Ephraim who?
A frame for your photograph.

Knock, knock.
Who's there?
Ezekiel.
Ezekiel who?
Easy keel to fit to a boat.

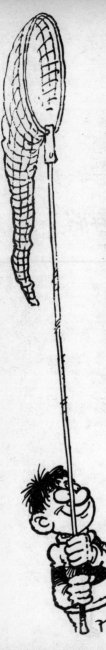

Knock, knock.
Who's there?
Matthew.
Matthew who?
Matthew always speak with that lisp?

Knock, knock.
Who's there?
Raphael.
Raphael who?
RAF ale is high-octane beer.

Knock, knock.
Who's there?
Stewart.
Stewart who?
Stew artistry by the chief chef.

Knock, knock.
Who's there?
Stephen.
Stephen who?
Steve entered every competition.

Knock, knock.
Who's there?
Jeremiah.
Jeremiah who?
Jerry, my ermine needs cleaning.

Knock, knock.
Who's there?
Alonso.
Alonso who?
Alone so long, I talk to myself.

Knock, knock.
Who's there?
Angus.
Angus who?
Angus us to see such cruelty.

Knock, knock.
Who's there?
Antonio.
Antonio who?
An' Tony owed even more.

HAMISH MACTOOTS SAYS:
DO I GET AN EXTRA FEE
FOR ALL THE WEE HOOTY
TOOTY JOKES ABOUT
US HAGGIS
CHUCKERS.

GLOO!

Knock, knock.
Who's there?
Archibald.
Archibald who?
Archie bald but Arthur wears a wig.

Knock, knock.
Who's there?
Bianca.
Bianca who?
Be anchored safely when storms blow up.

Knock, knock.
Who's there?
Blanche.
Blanche who?
Blanche-manager turned very pale.

Knock, knock.
Who's there?
Cordelia.
Cordelia who?
Could 'e leer more horribly?

Knock, knock.
Who's there?
Dolly.
Dolly who?
Dollicious food in this restaurant.

Knock, knock.
Who's there?
Cressida.
Cressida who?
Cress 'id 'er feet as she paddled in the river.

Knock, knock.
Who's there?
Curtis.
Curtis who?
Courtesy is a sign of good upbringing.

Knock, knock.
Who's there?
Edgar.
Edgar who?
'Ead gardener should be able to mow the lawn.

Knock, knock.
Who's there?
Elizabeth.
Elizabeth who?
I lose a bet every time I back a horse.

Knock, knock.
Who's there?
Francisco.
Francisco who?
Fancy 'is combing his hair backwards.

Knock, knock.
Who's there?
Owen.
Owen who?
Owen up, you did it.

Knock, knock.
Who's there?
Ellen.
Ellen who?
Elementary, my dear Watson.

Knock, knock.
Who's there?
Hermia.
Hermia who?
Her, me and you

Knock, knock.
Who's there?
Hermione.
Hermione who?
Her eye on me all the time?

Knock, knock.
Who's there?
Margery.
Margery who?
Ma geriatric these days.

Knock, knock.
Who's there?
Julius.
Julius who?
Duly ushered into the room.

Knock, knock.
Who's there?
Katharine.
Katharine who?
Katharine together for a social evening.

Knock, knock.
Who's there?
Macbeth.
Macbeth who?
Macbether now, thank you.

Knock, knock.
Who's there?
Lavinia.
Lavinia who?
Lavinia the way that I do.

Knock, knock.
Who's there?
Clifford.
Clifford who?
Cliff ordered jelly and got trifle.

Knock, knock.
Who's there?
Ross.
Ross who?
Rustle up a few more people.

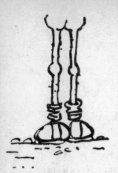

Knock, knock.
Who's there?
Talbot.
Talbot who?
Tall but too thin.

Knock, knock.
Who's there?
Lucy.
Lucy who?
Loose elastic can let you down.

Knock, knock.
Who's there?
Lucetta.
Lucetta who?
Lou set a difficult problem.

Knock, knock.
Who's there?
Lysander.
Lysander who?
Lies – and only a few are white ones.

Knock, knock.
Who's there?
Marcus.
Marcus who?
Mark us in, I've forgotten my pen.

Knock, knock.
Who's there?
Maria.
Maria who?
Ma real name is Mary.

Knock, knock.
Who's there?
Mariana.
Mariana who?
Marry on a sunny day in June.

Knock, knock.
Who's there?
Mortimer.
Mortimer who?
More timid than a bird.

Knock, knock.
Who's there?
Morton.
Morton who?
More turn to the right.

Knock, knock.
Who's there?
Oliver.
Oliver who?
A liver-and-bacon meal.

Knock, knock.
Who's there?
Olivia.
Olivia who?
Oh, live 'ere do you?

Knock, knock.
Who's there?
Orlando.
Orlando who?
All 'and over your valuables.

Knock, knock.
Who's there?
Orsino.
Orsino who?
'Orse in nobleman's stables.

Knock, knock.
Who's there?
Oswald.
Oswald who?
Oswald in like an old garden.

Knock, knock.
Who's there?
Othello.
Othello who?
A fellow I wouldn't trust an inch.

Knock, knock.
Who's there?
Paulina.
Paulina who?
Poor Lena is totally broke.

Knock, knock.
Who's there?
Pedro.
Pedro who?
Pedrol prices keep rising.

Knock, knock.
Who's there?
Puck.
Puck who?
Puck up your troubles in your old kitbag.

Knock, knock.
Who's there?
Rosaline.
Rosaline who?
Rozzer leaning on a lamp-post.

Knock, knock.
Who's there?
Sebastian.
Sebastian who?
Sebastian any other vehicle on the road.

Knock, knock.
Who's there?
Toby.
Toby who?
To be or not to be.

Knock, knock.
Who's there?
Stefan.
Stefan who?
Stefaning when he plays the drums.

Knock, knock.
Who's there?
Theseus.
Theseus who?
This useless idiot.

Knock, knock.
Who's there?
Thisbe.
Thisbe who?
This beef is too tough.

Knock, knock.
Who's there?
Vernon.
Vernon who?
Ver-non-smokers only, this carriage.

Knock, knock.
Who's there?
Viola.
Viola who?
Ve 'oller when 'urt.

Knock, knock.
Who's there?
Marcia.
Marcia who?
Ma, see a sight for sore eyes.

Knock, knock.
Who's there?
Marsha.
Marsha who?
Martians have landed.

Knock, knock.
Who's there?
Natasha.
Natasha who?
Not a shirt I'd wear.

Knock, knock.
Who's there?
Abby.
Abby who?
Abby go lucky.

Knock, knock.
Who's there?
Adelaide.
Adelaide who?
'Ad 'e laid an egg, you would have been surprised!

Knock, knock.
Who's there?
Edie.
Edie who?
Edie come, edie go.

Knock, knock.
Who's there?
Adolph.
Adolph who?
A dolphin is an intelligent creature.

Knock, knock.
Who's there?
Nesta.
Nesta who?
Nasturtiums are garden flowers.

Knock, knock.
Who's there?
Alastair.
Alastair who?
Alas, tearing about achieves nothing.

Knock, knock.
Who's there?
Sandy.
Sandy who?
'Sandeniably true.

THIS LAST JOKE PROVES IT'S A SCOTS JOKE BOOK!

I RENAME THIS BOOK 'SMART ALEC'S JOKE BOOK!'

Knock, knock.
Who's there?
Alfie.
Alfie who?
I'll feed the ducks if I want to.

Knock, knock.
Who's there?
Algy.
Algy who?
I'll gee up a slow horse.

Knock, knock.
Who's there?
Ellie.
Ellie who?
'Elicopters elevate vertically.

Knock, knock.
Who's there?
Elsie.
Elsie who?
I'll see you in my dreams.

Knock, knock.
Who's there?
Aloysius.
Aloysius who?
'Allo, is 'e ushering us out?

Knock, knock.
Who's there?
Alphonse.
Alphonse who?
I'll fancy my chances of winning.

Knock, knock.
Who's there?
Amadeus.
Amadeus who?
A mad use to put it to.

Knock, knock.
Who's there?
Ambrose.
Ambrose who?
'Am bones and pigs' trotters.

Knock, knock.
Who's there?
Nina.
Nina who?
Knee nerve causes knee jerk.

Knock, knock.
Who's there?
Ninette.
Ninette who?
Knee nettle-rash is irritating.

Knock, knock.
Who's there?
Nanette.
Nanette who?
None ate any of it.

Knock, knock.
Who's there?
Augustine.
Augustine who?
August in Spain is too hot.

Knock, knock.
Who's there?
Antoinette.
Antoinette who?
An' twine it round your finger.

Knock, knock.
Who's there?
Belle.
Belle who?
Bell-bottom trousers for a sailor.

Knock, knock.
Who's there?
Bettina.
Bettina who?
Bet in a casino on roulette.

DONG!
DONG!

Knock, knock.
Who's there?
Bella.
Bella who?
Bellicose and belligerent.

Knock, knock.
Who's there?
Benny.
Benny who?
Benny for your thoughts.

Knock, knock.
Who's there?
Penny.
Penny who?
Penny-pinching people.

Knock, knock.
Who's there?
Bernadette.
Bernadette who?
Bernard ate more than was good for him.

Knock, knock.
Who's there?
Beryl.
Beryl who?
Berilliant to have thought of it.

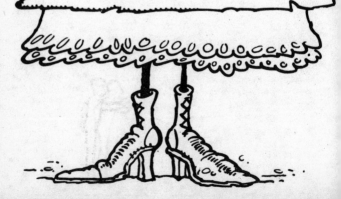

Knock, knock.
Who's there?
Betty.
Betty who?
Betticoats should not show below frocks.

Knock, knock.
Who's there?
Biddy.
Biddy who?
Biddy you had to leave so early.

Knock, knock.
Who's there?
Blodwen.
Blodwen who?
Blood when cut is normal.

Knock, knock.
Who's there?
Boris.
Boris who?
Boristol City or Boristol Rovers?

AND NOW FOR MY NEXT TRICK!

Knock, knock.
Who's there?
Brenda.
Brenda who?
Be rendered immobile by gout.

Knock, knock.
Who's there?
Brigid.
Brigid who?
Be rigid in your beliefs and standards.

Knock, knock.
Who's there?
Bronwen.
Bronwen who?
Brown when returning from holiday.

Knock, knock.
Who's there?
Bruce.
Bruce who?
Bruce easily with soft skin.

Knock, knock.
Who's there?
Bruno.
Bruno who?
Brew no more tea for me.

Knock, knock.
Who's there?
Candida.
Candida who?
Candida's capital is Ottawa.

Knock, knock.
Who's there?
Carlotta.
Carlotta who?
Car lot a use with no wheels!

Knock, knock.
Who's there?
Carmel.
Carmel who?
Car melted down for scrap metal.

Knock, knock.
Who's there?
Carol.
Carol who?
Carolina North or Carolina South?

Knock, knock.
Who's there?
Katerina.
Katerina who?
Cater in a small house for a hundred guests?

Knock, knock.
Who's there?
Cecily.
Cecily who?
Cecily is an island in the Mediterranean.

Knock, knock.
Who's there?
Cissie.
Cissie who?
Says 'e never went near the place.

Knock, knock.
Who's there?
Celestine.
Celestine who?
Cellars Tina explored.

Knock, knock.
Who's there?
Carlos.
Carlos who?
Carlossal cheek to do such a thing.

Knock, knock.
Who's there?
Clara.
Clara who?
Clara in broad daylight.

Knock, knock.
Who's there?
Colette.
Colette who?
Collections of stamps may be valuable.

Knock, knock.
Who's there?
Connie.
Connie who?
Connemara is in Ireland.

Knock, knock.
Who's there?
Carla.
Carla who?
Call 'er and she never hears.

Knock, knock.
Who's there?
Merle.
Merle who?
Merliciously intended.

Knock, knock.
Who's there?
Cosmo.
Cosmo who?
'Cos most people are like that.

Knock, knock.
Who's there?
Craig.
Craig who?
Craigy mountain ranges.

Knock, knock.
Who's there?
Crispin.
Crispin who?
Crisp inside, soggy outside.

Knock, knock.
Who's there?
Tom Sawyer.
Tom Sawyer who?
Tom saw yer at it again.

Knock, knock.
Who's there?
Cyril.
Cyril who?
Sir ill? Send him a get-well card.

Knock, knock.
Who's there?
Cyrus.
Cyrus who?
Sigh, rush about and get nowhere.

Knock, knock.
Who's there?
Vida.
Vida who?
Vee'd a veek off sick.

Knock, knock.
Who's there?
Delia.
Delia who?
Deal yer cards more openly.

Knock, knock.
Who's there?
Derek.
Derek who?
Directly across the road.

Knock, knock.
Who's there?
Dick.
Dick who?
Decapitated by the guillotine.

Knock, knock.
Who's there?
Dilys.
Dilys who?
Delicious food.

Knock, knock.
Who's there?
Dinah.
Dinah who?
Dai nurtured Welsh sheep.

Knock, knock.
Who's there?
Lola.
Lola who?
Lowland and highland.

Knock, knock.
Who's there?
Donna.
Donna who?
Don a different hat for rainy weather.

Knock, knock.
Who's there?
Doll.
Doll who?
Doll and wet all day.

Knock, knock.
Who's there?
Eamon.
Eamon who?
Eamon to please at all times.

Knock, knock.
Who's there?
Vera Lynn.
Vera who?
Vera Lynn concerto by Beethoven.

Knock, knock.
Who's there?
Earl.
Earl who?
Earl abuse and you'll get more in return.

Knock, knock.
Who's there?
Effie.
Effie who?
Effie can't do better, sack 'im.

Knock, knock.
Who's there?
Eli.
Eli who?
'E lied to me when he said that.

Knock, knock.
Who's there?
Betsy.
Betsy who?
Bets easily won.

Knock, knock.
Who's there?
Libby.
Libby who?
Liberty, equality, fraternity.

Knock, knock.
Who's there?
Elmer.
Elmer who?
Elm Ernie chopped down.

Knock, knock.
Who's there?
Emma.
Emma who?
Emerging from thick fog.

Knock, knock.
Who's there?
Emrys.
Emrys who?
Emrisking everything for your sake.

Knock, knock.
Who's there?
Erasmus.
Erasmus who?
Errors must be corrected.

Knock, knock.
Who's there?
Rastus.
Rastus who?
Raced us round the houses.

Knock, knock.
Who's there?
Ermintrude.
Ermintrude who?
'Er man too rude to my man.

Knock, knock.
Who's there?
Ernestine.
Ernestine who?
'Er nestin' box is full of eggs.

Knock, knock.
Who's there?
Esmeralda.
Esmeralda who?
As more 'eld 'er, she quietened down.

Knock, knock.
Who's there?
Hester.
Hester who?
Hesterically amusing.

Knock, knock.
Who's there?
Etta.
Etta who?
Ate a lot.

Knock, knock.
Who's there?
Rabbie.
Rabbie who?
Rabbiting on again.

```
DISCLAIMER

The publishers of this book
wish to draw a veil over the
disgraceful goings-on that
follow. H. MacToot and
PC49½ have both been charged
with disturbing the peace
and bound over to keep the
peace for two more joke books.
```

Knock, knock.
Who's there?
Robina.
Robina who?
Robina or Lucozade for you?

Knock, knock.
Who's there?
Rita.
Rita who?
Retarded or acting stupid?

Knock, knock.
Who's there?
Rhys.
Rhys who?
Risky to cross the road here.

Knock, knock.
Who's there?
Rees.
Rees who?
Resembles a monkey.

Knock, knock.
Who's there?
Rex.
Rex who?
Wrecks may be full of sunken treasure.

Knock, knock.
Who's there?
Raoul.
Raoul who?
Railwaymen having a kip on the sleepers.

Knock, knock.
Who's there?
Quintin.
Quintin who?
Quintin through a keyhole again?

Knock, knock.
Who's there?
Piers.
Piers who?
Peers through his specs.

Knock, knock.
Who's there?
Paddy.
Paddy who?
Padded about like a caged beast.

Knock, knock.
Who's there?
Pamela.
Pamela who?
Pommel 'er into slimness.

Knock, knock.
Who's there?
Olympia.
Olympia who?
I'll limp 'ere if I can't run.

Knock, knock.
Who's there?
Odette.
Odette who?
A debt I can't repay.

Knock, knock.
Who's there?
Noel.
Noel who?
No elevator working.

Knock, knock.
Who's there?
Theresa.
Theresa who?
Trees are chopped up for firewood.

Knock, knock.
Who's there?
Thelma.
Thelma who?
Thel Ma I've gone round to the shop.

Knock, knock.
Who's there?
Tabitha.
Tabitha who?
To beat 'er, you'll have to cheat.

Knock, knock.
Who's there?
Taffy.
Taffy who?
Taffy-nosed Welshman.

Knock, knock.
Who's there?
Stanislas.
Stanislas who?
Stan is last up every morning.

Knock, knock.
Who's there?
Sophia.
Sophia who?
So fear can cause panic.

Knock, knock.
Who's there?
Sonia.
Sonia who?
'S on yer conscience if you lie.

Knock, knock.
Who's there?
Shane.
Shane who?
Shane and shenshible.

Knock, knock.
Who's there?
Sydney.
Sydney who?
Sydneyly he left the room.

Knock, knock.
Who's there?
Sheila.
Sheila who?
She lurks round corners.

Knock, knock.
Who's there?
Sheena.
Sheena who?
Sheen a pair of shocks around?

BOI JABBERS— AN OIRISH JOKE!

Knock, knock.
Who's there?
Shamus.
Shamus who?
Shame us into confessing.

Knock, knock.
Who's there?
Sancho.
Sancho who?
'S anchovy spread I like best.

Knock, knock.
Who's there?
Pancho.
Pancho who?
Panchomime time is Christmas-time.

Knock, knock.
Who's there?
Salome.
Salome who?
So loan me a fiver.

PLUCK!

Knock, knock.
Who's there?
Rowena.
Rowena who?
Row enough to make your back ache.

Knock, knock.
Who's there?
Rory.
Rory who?
Raw realism on TV?

Knock, knock.
Who's there?
Rolf.
Rolf who?
Roll for a six on the dice.

Knock, knock.
Who's there?
Rodney.
Rodney who?
Rod needed for fishmerman.

Knock, knock.
Who's there?
Gary.
Gary who?
Gary on, sergeant-major.

Knock, knock.
Who's there?
Roddy.
Roddy who?
Roddy rotten trick to play on anyone.

Knock, knock.
Who's there?
Abner.
Abner who?
Ab nerve enough for anything.

Knock, knock.
Who's there?
Ben Hur.
Ben Hur who?
Ben hurt by cruel jokes?

Knock, knock.
Who's there?
Ezra.
Ezra who?
As rapid as possible.

Knock, knock.
Who's there?
Felix.
Felix who?
Flicks are movies.

Knock, knock.
Who's there?
Hagar.
Hagar who?
Hey guard, when's this train leaving?

Knock, knock.
Who's there?
Hermes.
Hermes who?
Her measles are very catching.

Knock, knock.
Who's there?
Herod.
Herod who?
Harrods is the top department store.

Knock, knock.
Who's there?
Ira.
Ira who?
'Ire a car and drive yourself.

Knock, knock.
Who's there?
Jonas.
Jonas who?
Joe gnashing his teeth with fury.

Knock, knock.
Who's there?
Joram.
Joram who?
Jor am time for bed.

Knock, knock.
Who's there?
Joseph.
Joseph who?
Joe's efficient at doing nothing.

Knock, knock.
Who's there?
Josiah.
Josiah who?
Joe's 'igher in the charts.

Knock, knock.
Who's there?
Justus.
Justus who?
Just as bad-tempered as ever.

Knock, knock.
Who's there?
Laban.
Laban who?
Lay banquets for thousands.

Knock, knock.
Who's there?
Lazarus.
Lazarus who?
Lasso us a couple of cows.

Knock, knock.
Who's there?
Lois.
Lois who?
Lowest of the low.

Knock, knock.
Who's there?
Lucas.
Lucas who?
Look as sweet as you can.

Knock, knock.
Who's there?
Martha.
Martha who?
Mar the ship for a hap'orth of tar.

*SEE"SMART ALEC'S BEASTLY JOKES FOR KIDS!"
  IT'S HORRID!!

WITHERED SHANKS EXPOSED TO THE FOUR WINDS

Knock, knock.
Who's there?
Mordecai.
Mordecai who?
More decay, said the dentist.

Knock, knock.
Who's there?
Narcissus.
Narcissus who?
Now scissors are safer than a penknife.

Knock, knock.
Who's there?
Nick.
Nick who?
Knickers need strong elastic.

Knock, knock.
Who's there?
Rod Stewart.
Rod Stewart who?
Rod's too artful by half.

Knock, knock.
Who's there?
Omar.
Omar who?
O ma beloved Papa.

Knock, knock.
Who's there?
Paulus.
Paulus who?
Paul us another couple of pints.

Knock, knock.
Who's there?
Perry.
Perry who?
Perilously close to the rocks.

Knock, knock.
Who's there?
Perez.
Perez who?
Peresent company excepted.

Knock, knock.
Who's there?
Sarah.
Sarah who?
Sarah doctor in the house?

Knock, knock.
Who's there?
Shadrach.
Shadrach who?
She'd wreck any car, the way she drives.

Knock, knock.
Who's there?
Sheba.
Sheba who?
Cheaper if you buy large quantities.

Knock, knock.
Who's there?
Shimben.
Shimben who?
Shimmy on until the small hours.

Knock, knock.
Who's there?
Tubal.
Tubal who?
Two balance on one bike?

Knock, knock.
Who's there?
Zachary.
Zachary who?
Zachary, dackory, dack, ducks do often quack.

Knock, knock.
Who's there?
Zebedee.
Zebedee who?
Ze birdies and the bees.

Knock, knock.
Who's there?
Patsy.
Patsy who?
P'haps he doesn't live here any more.

Knock, knock.
Who's there?
Mrs.
Mrs. who?
Misses Mother's apple-pie.

Knock, knock.
Who's there?
Mister.
Mister who?
Missed a bus and had to walk.

Knock, knock.
Who's there?
Aunt.
Aunt who?
Aren't your eyes a beautiful blue.

Knock, knock.
Who's there?
Madame.
Madame who?
Ma damn matches are too damp to strike.

Knock, knock.
Who's there?
Mamma.
Mamma who?
Murmur sweet nothings to me.

Knock, knock.
Who's there?
Widow.
Widow who?
Wid only a pension to live on.

Knock, knock.
Who's there?
Uncle.
Uncle who?
Uncalled for remarks.

Knock, knock.
Who's there?
Anson.
Anson who?
'Andsome is as 'andsome does.

Knock, knock.
Who's there?
Blake.
Blake who?
Blake and white.

Knock, knock.
Who's there?
Drake.
Drake who?
D'rake the leaves off the lawn?

Knock, knock.
Who's there?
Scott.
Scott who?
'S got to be a better way of doing it.

Knock, knock.
Who's there?
Fraser.
Fraser who?
Fr'e's a jolly good fellow.

Knock, knock.
Who's there?
Howard.
Howard who?
How 'ard are diamonds?

I QUITE AGREE

Knock, knock.
Who's there?
Ramsey.
Ramsey who?
Rams easily controlled by dogs.

Knock, knock.
Who's there?
Seymour.
Seymour who?
See more if you stand on the wall.

Knock, knock.
Who's there?
Warren.
Warren who?
War and Peace by Tolstoy.

Knock, knock.
Who's there?
Coco.
Coco who?
Coke only in this furnace.

Knock, knock.
Who's there?
Davis.
Davis who?
Day visitors and night callers.

Knock, knock.
Who's there?
Serge.
Serge who?
Search high and low.

Knock, knock.
Who's there?
Corporal.
Corporal who?
Cor, Pearl is beautiful.

Knock, knock.
Who's there?
Sergeant.
Sergeant who?
So gently does it.

Knock, knock.
Who's there?
Conway.
Conway who?
Gone way off the beaten track.

Knock, knock.
Who's there?
Hudson.
Hudson who?
Had sons and daughters.

Knock, knock.
Who's there?
Marco Polo.
Marco Polo who?
Mark a polling card with a cross.

Knock, knock.
Who's there?
Mungo Park.
Mungo Park who?
Mum go parking on yellow lines?

Knock, knock.
Who's there?
Landor.
Landor who?
Land ought to belong to everyone.

Knock, knock.
Who's there?
Lewis.
Lewis who?
Lewest form of human life.

Knock, knock.
Who's there?
Duff.
Duff who?
Duffeningly loud, that disco.

Knock, knock.
Who's there?
Hart.
Hart who?
Hearty greetings to all the family.

Knock, knock.
Who's there?
Monro.
Monro who?
Man rowing in a boat.

Knock, knock.
Who's there?
Nye.
Nye who?
Nice work if you can get it.

Knock, knock.
Who's there?
Wolfe.
Wolfe who?
Wool fez for your head in the Med.

Knock, knock.
Who's there?
Harris.
Harris who?
Harassed by people claiming money.

Knock, knock.
Who's there?
Hunter.
Hunter who?
Hun turned stone.

Knock, knock.
Who's there?
Murray.
Murray who?
Murray Christmas to one and all.

Knock, knock.
Who's there?
Wilson.
Wilson who?
Will Sonia be among the guests?

Knock, knock.
Who's there?
Bradley.
Bradley who?
Bradley in need of repair.

Knock, knock.
Who's there?
Gonzalez.
Gonzalez who?
Gone senseless after a knock-out.

Knock, knock.
Who's there?
Sherman.
Sherman who?
Shermany is split into West and East.

Knock, knock.
Who's there?
Tito.
Tito who?
Teetotal people don't drink alcohol.

SHATTERED UNDIES

Knock, knock.
Who's there?
Lenin.
Lenin who?
Linen should not be washed in public.

Knock, knock.
Who's there?
Castro.
Castro who?
Castronomical achievements by the chef.

Knock, knock.
Who's there?
Stalin.
Stalin who?
Star Linda saw through a telescope.

Knock, knock.
Who's there?
Asquith.
Asquith who?
As squiffy as usual.

Knock, knock.
Who's there?
Russ.
Russ who?
Russian tea contains a slice of lemon.

Knock, knock.
Who's there?
Russell.
Russell who?
Rustle of a bustle on an old dress.

Knock, knock.
Who's there?
Lester.
Lester who?
Less turkey, more chicken.

Knock, knock.
Who's there?
Dali.
Dali who?
Dali papers and weekly magazines.

GOODBYE
SOCK

Knock, knock.
Who's there?
Watt.
Watt who?
Watt a carry-on.

Knock, knock.
Who's there?
Ward.
Ward who?
Woah, dere, Dobbin.

Knock, knock.
Who's there?
Brett.
Brett who?
Bretter late than never.

Knock, knock.
Who's there?
Brock.
Brock who?
Brockfast in bed.

Knock, knock.
Who's there?
Cohen.
Cohen who?
Cohen, cohen, gone.

Knock, knock.
Who's there?
Dixon.
Dixon who?
Dictionaries make dull reading.

Knock, knock.
Who's there?
Giles.
Giles who?
Child's play, that's what it is.

Knock, knock.
Who's there?
Mason.
Mason who?
Mace on and my daughter.

EYE
EYE

Knock, knock.
Who's there?
Unwin.
Unwin who?
Unwinking with a glass eye.

Knock, knock.
Who's there?
Wyatt.
Wyatt who?
Y at the end of the alphabet, almost.

Knock, knock.
Who's there?
Archer.
Archer who?
Are churns still used to put milk in?

Knock, knock.
Who's there?
Ashton.
Ashton who?
Ash turned out of the grate.

Knock, knock.
Who's there?
Benson.
Benson who?
Ben's on another bender.

Knock, knock.
Who's there?
Foster.
Foster who?
Fussed 'er into making errors.

Knock, knock.
Who's there?
Holmes.
Holmes who?
Holmes fit for heroes to live in.

Knock, knock.
Who's there?
Martin.
Martin who?
Ma tun of sweets has gone.

Knock, knock.
Who's there?
Marietta.
Marietta who?
Marie ate 'er meal too fast and was ill.

Knock, knock.
Who's there?
Nola.
Nola who?
No learner may drive a car alone.

Knock, knock.
Who's there?
Todd.
Todd who?
Toddle off and don't come back.

Knock, knock.
Who's there?
Allen.
Allen who?
A lender may find he doesn't get things back.

Knock, knock.
Who's there?
Chico.
Chico who?
She coaxed me into agreeing.

Knock, knock.
Who's there?
Morley.
Morley who?
More leaves in summer than winter.

Knock, knock.
Who's there?
Olsen.
Olsen who?
All sentries have to be on their guard.

Knock, knock.
Who's there?
Palmer.
Palmer who?
Pa, Ma and Uncle Bill.

Knock, knock.
Who's there?
Parker.
Parker who?
Park early to be sure of a space.

Knock, knock.
Who's there?
Manuel.
Manuel who?
Man you elderly ladies like.

Knock, knock.
Who's there?
Lambert.
Lambert who?
Lambeth Palace is the home of the Archbishop.

Knock, knock.
Who's there?
Osborne.
Osborne who?
Is borne out by the evidence.

Knock, knock.
Who's there?
Webster.
Webster who?
Webs, to spiders, are easily spun.

Knock, knock.
Who's there?
Marshal.
Marshal who?
Martial arts can be dangerous.

Knock, knock.
Who's there?
Carey.
Carey who?
Care 'e took in writing a book.

Knock, knock.
Who's there?
Ellis.
Ellis who?
'Ell is down under.

Knock, knock.
Who's there?
Lever.
Lever who?
Leave a drop for me.

Knock, knock.
Who's there?
Irving.
Irving who?
'Er vinger is always wagging.

Knock, knock.
Who's there?
Jerome.
Jerome who?
D'yer roam around like a lost soul?

Knock, knock.
Who's there?
Marcel.
Marcel who?
Marceltoe, yew and holly.

Knock, knock.
Who's there?
Boswell.
Boswell who?
Boss well but his secretary off sick.

Knock, knock.
Who's there?
Hal.
Hal who?
Hal for leather.

Knock, knock.
Who's there?
Berta.
Berta who?
Berta your bread on both sides?

Knock, knock.
Who's there?
Osman.
Osman who?
Os many as possible.

Knock, knock.
Who's there?
Topas.
Topas who?
Tow passengers away in a broken-down car.

ZONK

Knock, knock.
Who's there?
Ulric.
Ulric who?
All rickety chairs to be sold.

Knock, knock.
Who's there?
Hassan.
Hassan who?
Has sanity totally vanished?

Knock, knock.
Who's there?
Horace.
Horace who?
Her race is for fillies only.

Knock, knock.
Who's there?
Malone.
Malone who?
M'lonely heart is aching.

Knock, knock.
Who's there?
Hartley.
Hartley who?
Hartley the right way to go about it.

Knock, knock.
Who's there?
Griselda.
Griselda who?
Chris elder than Liz?

Knock, knock.
Who's there?
Michelle.
Michelle who?
Me sheltering from the storm.

Knock, knock.
Who's there?
Toots.
Toots who?
Two's company, three's a crowd.

THROBBING MIT

Knock, knock.
Who's there?
Madeline.
Madeline who?
Madeline with things that don't concern you?

Knock, knock.
Who's there?
Muriel.
Muriel who?
Muriel painting on walls.

Knock, knock.
Who's there?
Theodosia.
Theodosia who?
Theo dozier than the other guy.

Knock, knock.
Who's there?
Thomasina.
Thomasina who?
Tom 'as seen a ghost by the look of him.

Knock, knock.
Who's there?
Hildegarde.
Hildegarde who?
Hilly garden means up and downs with the mower.

Knock, knock.
Who's there?
Billy Jo.
Billy who?
Billy joke with a billy-goat?

BUT I THOUGHT GOATS LIKED WEARING DRESSES

Knock, knock.
Who's there?
Ivy.
Ivy who?
I vish you vas vealthy.

Knock, knock.
Who's there?
Washington.
Washington who?
Washing turns and tumbles in the spin-drier.

Knock, knock.
Who's there?
Llewellyn.
Llewellyn who?
Lou well in with the management.

Knock, knock.
Who's there?
Norris.
Norris who?
No risk when you play safe.

Knock, knock.
Who's there?
Tobias.
Tobias who?
To buy us presents will cost a lot of money.

Knock, knock.
Who's there?
Hugh.
Hugh who?
Hugh too can have a body like mine.

Knock, knock.
Who's there?
Ivo.
Ivo who?
I vote we all go home. *So do I!*

Knock, knock.
Who's there?
Jay.
Jay who?
Jail-birds are convicts.

Knock, knock.
Who's there?
Jem.
Jem who?
Gemstones set in silver.

Knock, knock.
Who's there?
Mac.
Mac who?
Mac way for a naval officer.

Knock, knock.
Who's there?
Ned.
Ned who?
'N education is what you should get at school.

Knock, knock.
Who's there?
Pan.
Pan who?
Pancakes need tossing on a Tuesday.

Knock, knock.
Who's there?
Tam.
Tam who?
Tamsels in distress.

Knock, knock.
Who's there?
Amos.
Amos who?
A most peculiar boy.

Knock, knock.
Who's there?
Axel.
Axel who?
Accelerate by putting your foot down.

Knock, knock.
Who's there?
Boyd.
Boyd who?
Buoyed up by water-wings.

that's
ME.
signed.
ALEC (SMART)

Knock, knock.
Who's there?
Duke.
Duke who?
D'you curtsey to a princess?

Knock, knock.
Who's there?
Ewan.
Ewan who?
You another without any money?

Knock, knock.
Who's there?
Evan.
Evan who?
Evan 'elp the sailors on a night like this.

ANOTHER
WELSH JOKE
LOOK YOU
BACH!

Knock, knock.
Who's there?
Ewen.
Ewen who?
You an' yours are dear to me.

Knock, knock.
Who's there?
Fitz.
Fitz who?
Fits where it touches.

Knock, knock.
Who's there?
Fritz.
Fritz who?
Fritz in with everything else.

Knock, knock.
Who's there?
Hans.
Hans who?
Hans, knees and boomps-a-daisy.

IT SHOULD BEE "HANDS - KNEES -
AND BOTTY - A - DAISY"
BUT PEOPLE DON'T LIKE ME
TO TALK ABOUT
BOTTIES.
SIGNED
S. ALEXANDER.
(ALIAS THE PURPLE FANTUM)!

Knock, knock.
Who's there?
Ifor.
Ifor who?
I, for one, am dead against it.

Knock, knock.
Who's there?
Ikey.
Ikey who?
I keep rabbits and hamsters.

Knock, knock.
Who's there?
Kemp.
Kemp who?
Kemping out in the fields?

Knock, knock.
Who's there?
Muir.
Muir who?
More sorrow than anger.

Knock, knock.
Who's there?
Alroy.
Alroy who?
All royals are called Your Highness.

Knock, knock.
Who's there?
Athol.
Athol who?
A tholid thump on the throat.

Knock, knock.
Who's there?
Aubyn.
Aubyn who?
Auburn hair is nearly ginger.

Knock, knock.
Who's there?
Candy.
Candy who?
Can depend on her.

Knock, knock.
Who's there?
Carew.
Carew who?
Carewsing down the river.

Knock, knock.
Who's there?
Darcy.
Darcy who?
Dare say we'll meet again.

Knock, knock.
Who's there?
Monty.
Monty who?
Monte Carlo or bust.

Knock, knock.
Who's there?
Johan.
Johan who?
You handsome beast.

Knock, knock.
Who's there?
Franz.
Franz who?
Four 'ands in 'armony.

Knock, knock.
Who's there?
Ewart.
Ewart who?
You artful dodger.

Knock, knock.
Who's there?
Eldon.
Eldon who?
'Eld on until help arrived.